The cost of sin

Mark A. Anderson

DEDICATION

I dedicate this book to all the loved ones that I lost, Father Floyd, Mother Catherine, Brother Alan. All my brothers and sisters as well as my children Mark and Athena

Last but not least, you the reader

1 THE CITY OF SODOM

We will start our story in the city of Sodom, which was one of five cities in the Plain of Sidim. The cities were very close to each other. The bible will speak of two cities, Sodom and Gomorrah but our story will just talk about Sodom since both cities were right next to each other and both cities had the same issues with miscreants, those that were total lawless and did what they wanted to whomever they wanted.

The following chapters will attempt to bring out the daily lives of the people that lived in the city and what they were doing that angered God so much that he had to smite them with fire and brimstone. Of course, all the characters will be fictional, one can only imagine how life was thousands of years ago, but I will try my best.

Sodom was not the only city that was destroyed and forgotten about. A more recent find was Pompeii.

Is it possible that there were many more cities destroyed than we know about. Pompeii similar to Sodom and Gomorrah was filled with ungodly behavior. The close by volcano Vesuvius erupted and spewed ten feet of ash over all the occupants burring the entire city for decades to come. Most of the occupants were preserved in the ash as they lived their daily life, just frozen in time until they were discovered. There were also complete continents that were destroyed we still don't know if they really existed but you have Atlantis and MU. The state of society as it is today makes you wonder if more cities will be destroyed some would say due to climate change, I am sure the scientist would concur, but is there a higher power involved, in such diseases as HIV.

2 LUST/SALEH

Saleh is a 21-year-old man that loves to dress like a woman, although back in that day it seems everyone wore dresses. He grew up in a family of incest, his parents and siblings had their way with him and he did with his younger siblings. As Saleh goes through his day, he meets up with a few friends to discuss what the day ahead will look like.

"Saleh, are you going to the orgy in the town square tonight?" Abeer asked. "I am not sure, the last time there were not enough young boys to pass around and too many girls were there."
"This time they brought in fresh meat from Gomorrah we may even find

some virgins."
"That is what they always promise, they take your money and have yet to produce any worthwhile product. You know it is just as easy to watch for when the school ends and just follow the fresh one's home."
"Well do what you want I am going to the orgy tonight."

3 GLUTTONY/AYESHA

Ayesha is a 25-year-old woman, she had always been chunky because her parents love chubby babies. Anything Ayesha wanted she got. Her family was well to do and spared no coins when it came to their darling daughter.

Not only did she feel hungry and always want more and more, she also had a taste for women and girls having sex with her she found all different ways to bribe them.

As Ayesha walks down the cobblestone streets the venders look up and cannot wait for her to stop by their stand, she seems to be the main person to keep them in business buying up all their sweets. Hands full Ayesha looks down and sees a young child begging for food. Although she could easily hand the child a piece of her treasure trove of sweetness, she quickly turns away and keeps on walking as if she never saw the child.

4 GREED/MOSTAFA

Mostafa is a very rich man. He got rich off the back of others. His greed has made him a very lonely man. Mostafa has spent his life building his fortune and all he made was enemies not even one true friend. He has a lot of people that try to find favor with him hoping to get something in return but he could not be bothered.

Mostafa rarely gets out of his house but one day he wanted to get some air so out he went., wearing old clothes so he would not be confused with someone that has money also feels it is a waste of money to buy clothes when he still has some he can wear. As he walks buy a beggar boy, he notices that the boy is blind, a passerby tosses a coin in the direction of the

boy.   The boy did not know the coin was there, Mostafa quickly ran and picked up the coin before the boy even knew there was a coin for him. Mostafa continued walking as if nothing happened.

5 LAZY/ELA

Ela is the daughter of the mayor she loves to boss people around and if they give her any trouble, she will tell her father and he will lock up that person. Ela uses the staff to fan her when she is hot and if she has to go anywhere, they will carry her on the litter. If she is at the market the slaves would have to get what she wants while she waits impatiently for them to bring it back and if it is wrong, she will send them back several times, sometimes even if it is right just so she can make them run back and forth. There are times she has the slaves whipped for no reason at all, just for her amusement.

6 ANGER/KHATIB.

Khatib is constantly angry, why you ask? Partly because he is always drunk. The alcohol makes him brave and he starts fights with everyone that even looks at him. This caused him to lose his wife and children, they moved to Gomorrah. Once Khatib sobors up he is as nice as he can be, that is if his hangover isn't giving him too much pain, or his bruises he received from the fight the night before.

7 ENVY/FAYEZ

Fayez is standing next to her two other friends watching as Manal walks by.

"Look at Manal, I bet she has a sugar daddy buying her all the new stuff she flaunts around in town." Fayez exclaimed.

"Yes, look at her smirking at us, just because she is young and beautiful, she was very lucky to find a guy in this town that actually likes women." Sana stated.

"Well, I am young and beautiful too!" Fayez stated, the other two girls broke out in laughter and then walked off.

8 PRIDE/AL ZUBI

Al Zubi is so full of himself. He carries around a mirror not only to look at himself but to see who is watching him as he walks down the street. Most of the locals look at him with lust, they all imagine getting him in their bedroom and having their way with him. Al Zubi thinks he is a gift from God.

9 ABRAHAM

God sent three angels, two of them were on a mission to investigate the cities of Sodom and Gomorrah. God needed to know how bad it really was in those cities. One angel visited Abraham. The angel told Abraham that the sinning was so great in both Sodom and Gomorrah that he was going to destroy the cities.

"But lord" Abraham stated as he was bowing down to the angel. My nephew Lot lives in Sodom and he is your servant, please do not destroy the cities!"

"Why destroy the wicket with the righteous there may be fifty righteous people in these towns.

"If you can find ten non sinners in Sodom, I will spare it." The angel replied. "As for Lot, we will spare him and his family, but they must leave before we can destroy the cities." The angel said.

10 LOT

Lot was waiting at the entrance gate of the Sodom when he saw the two angels' approach. He immediately bowed down to them.

"Please come with me to my house for you may wash up and sleep the night there under my protection." Lot said to the angels.

"No thank you, we will merely sleep in the streets" The angel answered. The angels were very adamant about not going to Lot's house. Lot continued to show the logic of them spending the night at his house, the angels gave in and followed him to his house.

"Tomorrow we will have to destroy these cities because they are filled with wickedness." The angels said to Lot.

"Please give me a chance to talk to two men that are promised to marry my daughters and see if I can convince them to come with us."

"We will grant you the time but if they stay, they will perish" Lot went to talk to the men and they only laughed at him thinking he was joking.

Lot prepared a feast for the angels after they ate, he asked them to lay down for the night. As soon as Lot had said that he could hear a ruckus outside of his house. Men from the town had found out that the angels were at Lot's house and they wanted to have sex with them. Young and old men showed up at Lot's house and angrily banged on Lot's door and demanded he send out the angel so they could rape them

"Please go away do not plan any wicked deeds with them. I have two daughters and they are virgins; they have never been with any men. Take them instead. Do to them what you feel you need to do, but leave these men alone." That angered the men even more as they tried to push their way into Lot's

house.

The angels grabbed Lot and pulled him into his house and then locked the door. The angels them blinded the men that were trying to break into the house so that they would not even be able to find the house.

The next morning the angels lead Lot, his two daughters and his wife out of town.

"One important thing, you must never look back at the town once we start destroying it. Lot, I want you to take your family up to the mountains, we have to make sure you and your family are safe before we can start."

"I cannot go to the mountains for I fear I will die."

"There is a small town close by called Zoar, it is a small town and will not be destroyed, go there."

Lot and his family started running to Zoar the sun began to rise and fire

and brimstone started raining down on the cities of Sodom and Gomorrah. Lot's wife heard the commotion from the heavens and stopped to look at the
cities.

This story came from Geneses chapter 18 and 19 and was created in a way I thought life may have been back in the day.

ABOUT THE AUTHOR

Mark A. Anderson was born in Wilkes-Barre, PA, he grew up in a haunted house which made the basis for his stories supernatural right at home. He started writing his first book "The Homza's Son" While in the Air Force and sitting in observation towers for 12 hours a day. Mark A. Anderson read a lot of hero comic books and Stephen King books which also gave him ideas for his books. Once "The Homza's Son" was finished he quickly started working on "He's Alive, BUT!" The sequel to "The Homza's Son" The last of the trilogy is: "Homza III".

With a young daughter at home Mark A. Anderson decided to start writing children books for her to read. "I'm A Bee" is her favorite. "Ma Ma, I'm Home" is a book of 4 short stories for tweens and "Stranger Danger" is a good teaching book to teach children about the dangers of strangers. "Do unto Others" basic rules about not bullying and other rules that are good to live by. "Strangers Live in the Darkness" Horror story for teens. Pick up Mark's autobiography "Who' Cares" to read more of Mark's life. Mark A. Anderson is also a paranormal Investigator. I co-wrote "Lion son the Run" with my daughter Athena. All books can be found on Amazon.